W9-CKI-131

Ohio

BY M. J. YORK

The Child's World

Published by The Child's World®
1980 Lookout Drive • Mankato, MN 56003-1705
800-599-READ • www.childsworld.com

ACKNOWLEDGMENTS
The Child's World®: Mary Berendes, Publishing Director
The Design Lab: Design and production
Red Line Editorial: Editorial direction

PHOTO CREDITS: Doug Lemke/Shutterstock Images, cover, 1, 3; Matt
Kania/Map Hero, Inc., 4, 5; Bryan Busovicki/iStockphoto, 7; Michael Ciu/
iStockphoto, 9; iStockphoto, 10; Diana Lundin/Bigstock, 11; Kiichiro Sato/AP
Images, 13, North Wind Picture Archives/Photolibrary, 15; Denise Kappa/
Shutterstock Images, 17; AP Images, 19; Photolibrary, 21; One Mile Up, 22;
Quarter-dollar coin image from the United States Mint, 22

LIBRARY OF CONGRESS CATALOGING-IN-PUBLICATION DATA
York, M. J., 1983–
  Ohio / by M.J. York.
    p. cm.
  Includes bibliographical references and index.
  ISBN 978-1-60253-479-7 (library bound : alk. paper)
  1. Ohio—Juvenile literature. I. Title.

F491.3.Y67 2010
977.1–dc22

                              2010018653

Printed in the United States of America in Mankato, Minnesota.
July 2010
F11538

On the cover:
Old Man's Cave
is a **popular**
area of Hocking
Hills State Park
in Ohio.

CONTENTS

Geography

Let's explore Ohio! Ohio is in the central United States. This area is called the Midwest. Lake Erie is north of Ohio.

Lake Erie is one of the five Great Lakes. The others are Lake Superior, Lake Michigan, Lake Huron, and Lake Ontario.

MICHIGAN

Lake
Erie

Toledo

Sandusky

Cleveland

Akron

Youngstown

PENNSYLVANIA

Canton

OHIO

New Philadelphia

Coshocton

Columbus

Springfield

Dayton

Marietta

Athens

INDIANA

Hamilton

Cincinnati

Serpent
Mound State
Memorial

NORTH
EAST
SOUTH
WEST

Ohio River

Ironton

WEST VIRGINIA

KENTUCKY

Cities

Columbus is the capital of Ohio. It is the largest city in the state. Cleveland, Cincinnati, and Toledo are other well-known cities.

More than 700,000 people live in Columbus. ▶

Land

Most of Ohio is hilly. Rolling hills are in the west. Rockier hills are in the east. The state also has many rivers and river **valleys**. The Ohio River is Ohio's southern border.

Much of Ohio's land is rich and good for farming. ▶

Plants and Animals

Hundreds of years ago, forests covered Ohio. The state tree of Ohio is the buckeye. Its nuts look like the eye of a male deer, or a buck. Ohio is called "the Buckeye State." Ohio's state bird is the cardinal. Cardinals live at the edge of forests. The state **mammal** is the white-tailed deer.

Buckeye trees produce large nuts. ▶

People and Work

Almost 11.5 million people live in Ohio. Many people work in **manufacturing**. They make cars, machines, **chemicals**, and food. Others work in mining and farming.

Ohio is known for its car manufacturing plants. ▶

History

Many Native American groups have lived in the Ohio area for thousands of years. People from Europe first visited the area in the 1600s. England and France fought over the land in the 1760s. England won. The United States took control of the land after that. Ohio became the seventeenth state on February 19, 1803.

The first white settlers in Ohio were farmers. In later years, more people worked in factories as roads and technology improved.

Early Ohio settlers built cabins from trees and farmed on the land. ▶

Ways of Life

Sports are popular in Ohio. The state has many **professional** and college sports teams. The first professional baseball team in the United States was the Cincinnati Red Stockings. The team began in 1869. They are now called the Reds. Many visitors come to Lake Erie. They boat and fish. They ride roller coasters at Cedar Point.

Water activities are popular in Ohio. ▶

Famous People

Seven U.S. presidents were born in Ohio. These include Ulysses S. Grant, Rutherford B. Hayes, and William McKinley. Neil Armstrong was also born here. He was the first person to walk on the moon. John Glenn, another **astronaut**, was born in Ohio, too.

Neil Armstrong walked on the moon on July 20, 1969. ▶

Famous Places

Ohio is known for Native American mounds that were built long ago. The huge Serpent Mound is almost a quarter of a mile (.4 km) long. It looks like a long snake. The Pro Football Hall of Fame is in Canton, Ohio. Visitors to Cleveland can also see the Rock and Roll Hall of Fame and **Museum**.

Visitors can see the Serpent Mound at the Serpent Mound State **Memorial**. ▶

State Symbols

Seal

Ohio's state seal shows a farm field with the rising sun. This shows the importance of farming in the state. Go to childsworld.com/links for a link to Ohio's state Web site, where you can get a firsthand look at the state seal.

Flag

Ohio's state flag is not a rectangle. It is shaped like a **pennant** with two points. The colors and the stars honor the United States. The red and white circle is the O in Ohio and also stands for a buckeye.

Quarter

Ohio's state quarter shows an astronaut and an early airplane. The quarter came out in 2002.

Glossary

astronaut (AS-truh-not): An astronaut is a person who goes into outer space. John Glenn is a former astronaut from Ohio.

chemicals (KEM-uh-kulz): Chemicals are substances used in chemistry. Some people in Ohio work to make chemicals.

mammal (MAM-ul): A mammal is a warm-blooded animal that has a backbone and hair; female mammals can produce milk to feed their babies. Ohio's state mammal is the white-tailed deer.

manufacturing (man-yuh-FAK-chur-ing): Manufacturing is the task of making items with machines. Many people work in manufacturing in Ohio.

memorial (muh-MOR-ee-ul): A memorial is a place or thing that honors people or events. The Serpent Mound State Memorial is in Ohio.

museum (myoo-ZEE-um): A museum is a place where people go to see art, history, or science displays. The Rock and Roll Hall of Fame and Museum is in Cleveland, Ohio.

pennant (PEN-int): A pennant is a flag in the shape of a triangle. Ohio's flag is shaped like a pennant with two points.

popular (POP-yuh-lur): To be popular is to be enjoyed by many people. Sports are popular in Ohio.

professional (pro-FESH-uh-nul): Professional means getting paid to do something that others do only for fun. Ohio has many professional sports teams.

seal (SEEL): A seal is a symbol a state uses for government business. Ohio's seal shows a farm.

symbols (SIM-bulz): Symbols are pictures or things that stand for something else. The seal and the flag are Ohio's symbols.

technology (tek-NAWL-uh-jee): Technology is scientific knowledge applied to practical things. As roads and technology improved, people in Ohio began to work in factories.

valleys (VAL-eez): Valleys are the low points between two mountains. Ohio has river valleys.

Further Information

Books

Keller, Laurie. *The Scrambled States of America*. New York: Henry Holt, 2002.

Schonberg, Marcia. *B is for Buckeye: An Ohio Alphabet*. Chelsea, MI: Sleeping Bear Press, 2000.

Schonberg, Marcia. *Cardinal Numbers: An Ohio Counting Book*. Chelsea, MI: Sleeping Bear Press, 2002.

Taylor-Butler, Christine. *Ohio*. New York: Children's Press, 2007.

Web Sites

Visit our Web site for links about Ohio:
childsworld.com/links

Note to Parents, Teachers, and Librarians: We routinely verify our Web links to make sure they are safe and active sites. So encourage your readers to check them out!

Index